Choices

Cindi Jasa

CHOICES

For publishing inquiries, contact:
YOLT Publishing
c/o CMI
13518 L Street
Omaha, NE 68137

ISBN: 978-0-9982931-4-1

Publishing and production services by Concierge Marketing Inc.

Library of Congress and Cataloging-in-Publication
data on file with the publisher

Printed in the USA
10 9 8 7 6 5 4 3 2

I dedicate this book to my oldest grandchildren, Eliza, Ethan and Caleb, who are now at this exciting time in their lives. I love you and I appreciate the wise choices you have made. I pray you will continue down this path.

I am also writing this book for my younger grandchildren, Emily, Evlyn, Zeke, Xander, Bri and Brynn, who aren't quite ready for all of this information but are closely watching the choices of those around them.

I have enjoyed watching all of you grow up (even though it is going by much too quickly!). I look forward to making many more memories with each of you!

I love you all so much!!

Contents

1

Introduction

I feel like I was challenged to write this book through a series of events. It wasn't in my original plan but I definitely see a need for it. If this book is in your hands right now, I believe it is there for a reason.

Life is full of choices and every day you make decisions that not only affect you for the present moment, but for eternity. With that in mind, it's best to carefully consider each choice you make and have the information needed to make the best choices possible. This book does not contain all the answers to the issues of life. It's just an invitation to consider the choices I am presenting to you.

I believe that your generation has been given much information regarding life and relationships that is not based on truth. Because of that, I would like to share some truth with you. That is why I decided to write this book. Some of you may already know the things I will be sharing but many of you do not. I ask you to consider the information I am presenting. I also encourage you to check out the facts for yourself to make sure that all I am telling you is true.

These are some of the most important years of your life. You will be faced with big choices that will affect the rest of your life. I'm sharing with you some of the things I wish someone had told me when I was your age. It would have changed the whole course of my life.

My first advice is to learn from the mistakes you see others make (starting with me). You don't have to follow the crowd. We all need someone to look up to – someone who will choose to be a leader and not a follower. I believe many are looking for a good example that they can imitate. You could choose to be that example and in doing so, it could change your life.

Foundation

"All who listen to My (Jesus') instructions and follow them are wise, like a man who builds his house on solid rock. Though the rain comes in torrents, and the floods rise and the storm winds beat against his house, it won't collapse, for it is built on rock. But those who hear My instructions and ignore them are foolish, like a man who builds his house on sand. For when the rains and floods come, and storm winds beat against his house, it will fall with a mighty crash." Matthew 7:24-27

You are now in the process of building your 'house', which is your life, and we all know that a good foundation is the best way to start the process.

I am wondering what your knowledge of God is at this point in your life? Is He someone you have heard about from other people or possibly in church, or is He someone you know personally? There's a really big difference between these two. I'm sure you probably know a lot of people but you most likely have only a few very close friends. Jesus wants to be your closest friend.

It's difficult to love God if you don't know Him and who He really is. Some people assume that His teachings aren't relevant today in our modern world but GOD IS LOVE and GOD LOVES YOU! This basic truth is a great foundation to build on because it will never change. It doesn't matter who you are or what you've done, God is passionately in love with you.

Let's go back to the very beginning of time. God existed before the world was created. Jesus, the Holy Spirit and the angels lived in heaven. Everything was perfect there. They didn't need anyone or anything to fulfill them. But God wanted to give His Son, Jesus, a family that would love Him.

God knew that when He created man, we would make the choice to sin and not be able to make it to heaven on our own. He determined to give us a free will and allow us to choose whether or not we would love Him. God knew that many would not choose Him, but true love can't be forced on a person. It has

to be their choice. Because God loved us so much, He had a solution in place before creation to save us from our sin if we would choose to follow His plan.

Jesus would have to come to earth, be born as a baby and live a perfect life – one without any sin. Then He would have to die the worst possible death (crucifixion) to pay the price for the sins we would commit. After three days He would rise and have victory over sin and death forever. It almost sounds too amazing to be true.

Perhaps you have heard a version of that story but have you ever stopped to really think about what it means? Jesus willingly gave up His crown and even His life because He thought you were worth it! He would have died for you even if you were the only person on earth. He loves you that much! Take some time to reflect on that.

The Bible says in Hebrews 12:2 that Jesus saw you from the cross, long before you were ever born, and He chose to die "For the joy that was set before Him". YOU were that joy! He loves you and there is nothing you can do to change how He feels about you. I bet you don't know anyone who loves you like that. Even the very best parents can fail in some ways, but God is patient. He will never fail you and He loves you through all the ups and downs of your life.

When the time came for you to be conceived, everything was planned out in advance (before the world we live in even existed). God chose your parents and your family. That may be a difficult idea

for some to comprehend. In today's society, there are many people who don't even know one or both of their birth parents. You may be one of those people.

You may have been told that your birth was a mistake but there is nothing further from the truth! God knew just when you would be born and He doesn't make any mistakes. He's in the business of turning our mistakes into His miracles. You just have to choose to believe the truth of how God really sees you.

What if you believed what I just told you? If God allowed you to be conceived by parents you may not know, what could possibly be the reason for that? God doesn't always give us the answers to these questions but He does promise that He will always be with us in whatever we face in life, and He can make ALL things work together for our good if we love Him.

God has special purposes and plans for your life that only you can fulfill. No one else is created exactly like you. But God won't force His will upon you, and He won't force you to love Him. Your parents and your family are all part of that plan and purpose.

One of God's commandments is to honor your father and your mother. That idea might be easier for some than for others. What if you don't think they deserve that? Don't they have to earn honor? Maybe one (or both) of your parents left (or died) when you were young and you don't have a relationship with them at all. You might not even know them if

you passed them on the street. Do you still have to honor your parents? God says 'YES', but why? Because God promises that if we honor them, we will live a long, blessed life. I think that sounds like a really good reason.

Have you ever considered that if you honor your parents just like they are, it could possibly change their heart towards you? On the other hand, honoring your parents might change your heart towards them.

Do you have siblings? How do you feel about them? Do you get along with each other or is there fighting, jealousy and envy? Do you wish the best for them or is it more of a competition? God tells us to love others and His desire is that you begin to live that love out in the family He chose to put you in.

Could it possibly be that God put you together in a family to teach you some things, like maybe how to love when it's not always easy? If you are more concerned with loving people outside of your family circle, maybe you need to go back and look at your own heart again. If you are really put in your family for a specific reason, what might God be trying to teach you? You may be convinced that you are just fine and it's the other person who has the real problem. But have you ever thought about how God might see your circumstances?

What would it look like if you truly loved your family, knowing there's a reason you were placed there? We all have things we can learn from each

other. Maybe you need to stop and simply ask God what He is trying to teach you. The truth is, God loves you so much that He will do whatever it takes to reach you. He will go to great lengths to get your attention. God's best for your life is that you will learn the lessons that will lead to good choices, otherwise the consequences of poor choices will have a negative impact on your whole life. If you are open to learning the things God is trying to teach you, it will change your life and the way you love others around you.

3

Friends

"A mirror reflects a man's face, but what he is really like is shown by the kind of friends he chooses."
Proverbs 27:19

"Stop being mean, bad-tempered and angry. Quarreling, harsh words, and dislike of others should have no place in your lives. Instead, be kind to each other, tender-hearted, forgiving one another, just as God has forgiven you because you belong to Christ."
Ephesians 4:31

I believe cultivating good friendships is another good foundation stone. Take a good look at who you have chosen to be your friends. I'm not talking about being kind to people in general. This is about the people you spend your time with. Bad company corrupts good morals. People identify you with the friends you choose. The more time you spend with these friends, chances are good you will become like them.

What kinds of things do you talk about? Where do you like to spend your free time? Are you and your friends holding each other accountable to high standards or are you choosing to settle for low standards? It's important to remember that every choice you make right now in these years will affect your future and eternity in some way. With that in mind, it would seem pretty crucial that you make choices that will have a positive effect later in your life.

I've heard stories about teens who did things they regretted, things that cost them more than they ever would have dreamed at the time. Some teens lost a college scholarship, made sexual choices that will stay with them forever, or possibly even had thoughts that led them to suicide. You might have a story of your own to add to this list.

I can't imagine how I would feel if I had been part of a group who teased or taunted someone to the point that they would want to take their own life. On the other hand, what if you were the one person who showed kindness and, without even knowing it, saved them from doing something drastic? I know which choice I want to make. How about you?

These years leading into adulthood can be very hard if you don't have the positive influence of good friends. When I say "good" friends, I'm talking about friends who have high standards and don't settle for a life lived without purpose.

It makes me sad to hear how people treat one another at times. Many times I think we may not take the time to consider that someone may be going through a very hard time and they could really use a friend at that moment.

Is gossip truly helpful? Would you want others to say the things about you that you say about them? If you put other people down, does it really make you look better? If you encourage others to have low standards, does that make what you do more acceptable?

Why is kindness so hard for some and yet so natural for others? Again, it comes down to a choice. You need to decide if you want to bring out the best or the worst in others, because what you do for them, they will most likely do for you. So it seems that a wise first choice is, "What kind of person do I want to be?"

Do you believe that simple acts of kindness could change the world (or at least change the world around you)? I encourage you to try it out and see what happens. I know that choosing to be kind would change you in a positive way, and that's a really good start!

I have tried for years to help people understand how rewarding kindness can be. It brings joy like nothing else I can compare to. It makes my day

when someone shares with me something positive they did for another person and how it affected their life and the lives of others.

When my oldest grandchildren were younger, we used to intentionally look for ways to be kind to people. We often chose to buy meals, open doors or just make the extra effort to treat others with respect. We enjoyed those times very much.

I love how my family looks for ways to show kindness, especially around the holidays. One Christmas we made tie blankets together and gave them to people who were hurting.

That same year my son's youth group for high school boys also made tie blankets. The boys selected people they knew personally to receive the blankets. Then they prayed for these people. The blankets touched the receivers and the givers alike - so much, in fact, that the boys asked to make blankets again the next Christmas. That youth group saw and experienced the benefits of kindness.

It encourages my heart when I see my family members reach out to others in many different ways. My sons, their wives and their children love to help others without receiving recognition. I am blessed abundantly when I hear about the things they do. I know that, in big and small ways, my family is making a difference in people's lives and in the world. Every one of them makes me proud!

You may have your own ideas about how you can impact others' lives through kindness. Be creative and have fun with it. I can promise you that your joy will increase!

4

Words

"A man's heart determines his speech. A good man's speech reveals the rich treasures within him." Matthew 12:34-35

"Don't use bad language. Say only what is good and helpful to those you are talking to, and what will give them a blessing." Ephesians 4:29

"You must give account on Judgment Day for every idle word you speak. Your words now reflect your fate then: either you will be justified by them or you will be condemned." Matthew 12:36-37

Have you ever stopped to listen to the words that come out of your mouth? What do your words say about your character in any given moment? I would simply ask you, "What kind of message are you sending to others"?

How do you use God's name? Is His name a curse word or a common term you throw around lightly, or do you speak it with reverence? Would others be drawn to God because of how you speak about Him?

How do you talk about yourself and other people? Do you chose positive words or do the words "stupid", "worthless" or "no good" come to mind? Do you know that your words have great power in heaven and on earth? We can cause things to happen, good or bad, just by the words we speak. If you remember, Jesus created the whole world with His words.

"For when He (Jesus) spoke, the world began!" Psalms 33:9

Have you ever said "That person really makes me mad?" I'm sure we've all had thoughts like this at some point, but I encourage you to think about what you are really saying. This statement gives the other person the power to control your emotions if you truly believe their actions can determine your response. How you respond to a situation is your choice. No one can actually 'make you mad' unless you let them. I read a sign once that said "No one can drive you crazy unless you give them the keys!" I encourage you to 'keep your keys' and take control of your emotions!

If you think you are being humble when you put yourself down, then let's examine what true humility looks like. When we are proud, we are thinking more highly of ourselves than we should. When we practice humility, we allow others to take the initiative in offering praise. It isn't necessary to boast about the good things we have done. Through humility, we realize that our lives have no real meaning without God. However, through a relationship with God, you have great worth and value and can then see yourself as God sees you.

God thinks you are amazing!! The Bible says that you are created in the image of God. He didn't make any mistakes when He created you and He wants you to believe that. Maybe you aren't the size or shape you would like to be, or you may not think you're as pretty or as handsome as some of the people you know. But outer appearance doesn't always reflect what is in the heart. A pure heart alone can make a person radiant and more attractive than natural beauty ever could.

We are told to praise God in ALL things. That includes the good times, the times we may see as 'bad', and everything in between. Praising God in all things simply means being thankful in whatever situations you are facing.

After working on the concept of "praising God in all things" for many years, I would think I'd have it down by now. I've decided it's a lifelong process. When I find myself being pulled down by the hard issues of life, I choose to thank God

for these difficult situations and especially for the good things He is accomplishing in my character through these hard times.

I had an interesting encounter at the airport recently. I was taken aside and put through a thorough search of myself and my belongings. It was very humiliating, especially since I knew I had done nothing wrong. They tested everything in my bag. It made me feel like a terrorist! I had just read a few books on praising God in every situation so I tried to put this in to practice in this uncomfortable situation.

When it was all over, I thought about what had happened and what I could possibly learn from it. I thought about how God treats me with love and kindness when I have disobeyed Him. He would never humiliate me or cause me to think that I am a bad person. He teaches and corrects me in ways that encourage me to do better while reminding me that He loves me. On the other hand, the devil tries to make me feel like a failure and wants to convince me that I will never change. He wants me to feel shame over what I have done.

It's important for me to realize that I'm not always where I need to be spiritually but that God won't stop working on me until I am where He needs me to be. I choose to be thankful for this because I want to be the best 'me' in God's eyes that I can possibly be.

Whether or not you like your parents or someone in your family, try to find reasons to thank God for each person. For example, without your parents, you

wouldn't have the gift of life. It may feel like a stretch to thank God, but I would encourage you to do it anyway. In time, you may find your attitudes toward your family start to change. Eventually, I believe your appreciation will become genuine and heartfelt.

Is there someone you find it hard to be around? Thank God for putting them in your life. It's hard to practice being kind and compassionate unless we have challenging people in our lives. It's also hard to be upset with them if you are thanking God for putting them there. Being around these people can reveal what is in our own heart. Think about it this way; when you are under pressure, how do you respond?

I don't know what you are facing right now in your life, but I sincerely ask you to try this approach. It's not a quick fix and your situation may or may not change right away, but it will change your heart. I know this for certain because I am on that journey myself. And if your heart changes, you may find that your circumstances and the people in your life don't seem so unbearable after all.

Remember that your words are so powerful that they either bring life or death to you, to others, and even to your circumstances. Choose your words wisely. Ask God to help you really listen to yourself and the words you speak. Words will literally change your life!

"Death and life are in the power of the tongue."
Proverbs 18:21

5

Suicide

"The Lord is close to those whose hearts are breaking." Psalms 34:18

"I cannot understand how you can bother with mere puny man, to pay any attention to him! And yet You have made him only a little lower than the angels, and placed a crown of glory and honor upon his head." Psalms 8:4-5

"What can we ever say to such wonderful things as these? If God is on our side, who can ever be against us?" Romans 8:31

What would ever make you think your life isn't worth living? I have to admit, I have taken that road before in my mind. That's when you need to stop, realize that your biggest enemy (the devil – yes, he's very real) is lying to you, and then take action against his lies. The way to do that is to replace those lies with the truth – what God says about you. Find God's words of encouragement and promises from the Bible and speak those words out loud. See how the atmosphere changes around you.

It may feel like the whole world is against you, but God is still for you (and His vote outweighs all others)! Allow God to be your best friend, and ask Him to provide someone in your life who can be the friend you need. God loves you so much more than you could ever dream or imagine! Allow His purposes to fill your life.

Whatever circumstances have brought you to this low point in your life will change over time if you keep moving forward. Maybe you are being bullied by people around you. At some point, those people will no longer be in your life. I believe the devil must know that God has a very special plan for you or he wouldn't be putting suicidal thoughts in your mind. The devil doesn't want you to fulfill God's plans because if you do, you could make a positive difference in the lives of others. If I had chosen suicide, I wouldn't be here writing this to you today. Make it your goal to please God and the devil will have to leave you alone!

I would like to share Psalm 31 with you. I hope it encourages you.

"I am radiant with joy because of your mercy, for You have listened to my troubles and have seen the crisis in my soul. You have not handed me over to my enemy, but have given me open ground in which to maneuver.

O Lord, have mercy on me in my anguish. My eyes are red from weeping; my health is broken from sorrow. I am pining away with grief; my years are shortened, drained away because of sadness. My sins have sapped my strength; I stoop with sorrow and with shame. I am scorned by all my enemies and even more by my neighbors and friends. They dread meeting me and look the other way when I go by. I am forgotten like a dead man, like a broken and discarded pot. I heard the lies about me, the slanders of my enemies. Everywhere I looked, I was afraid, for they were plotting against my life.

But I was trusting You, O Lord, I said, 'You alone are my God; my times are in Your hands. Rescue me from those who hunt me down relentlessly. Let Your favor shine again upon Your servant; save me just because You are so kind!' Don't disgrace me, Lord, by not replying when I call to You for aid.

Hide Your loved ones in the shelter of Your presence, safe beneath Your hand, safe from all conspiring men. Blessed is the Lord, for He has shown me that His never-failing love protects me like the walls of a fort!"

The Lord protects those He loves, and God loves YOU! So be encouraged and depend on the Lord to help you. He will not let you down!

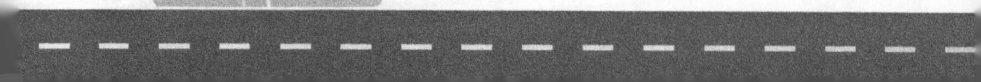

⟨6⟩

Entertainment

"I will walk within my house in the integrity of my heart. I will set no worthless thing before my eyes." Psalms 101:2-3

"Determination to be wise is the first step toward becoming wise! And with your wisdom, develop common sense and good judgment." Proverbs 4:7

Do you have boundaries set for yourself about what you allow to come into your mind? Our minds and our thoughts influence everything we say and do. That's why it's so important to guard our minds.

Think about a typical week for you. Do you like to go to movies? What is your standard there? Does the sexual content and bad language bother you or have you come to expect it? Do you choose movies with caution because of what you might see, or are you just looking to entertain yourself?

Years ago, I realized that PG-13 movies can sometimes be the most offensive ones. They almost always contain sexual content. Does it ever make you uncomfortable when you are watching one of these movies with someone of the opposite sex? If not, do you ever question why it doesn't? Do you ever watch inappropriate movies at home by yourself? What choices are the people in the movies making? Do their choices line up with what you believe to be right?

I encourage you to think about everything you put in front of your eyes. Every time you look at something that is inappropriate, you become a little less sensitive to seeing it the next time. After a while, you can become desensitized to something that would have previously disturbed you. How sensitive is your spirit to what you see?

We can shut out that inner voice of the Holy Spirit (some might call it conscience) by continuing to make unwise choices. If we tune God out long enough, we may eventually lose sight of what is right and what is wrong.

What music do you like? Does it leave you with positive or negative thoughts? Every song contains a message. Do you choose to listen to music with

uplifting lyrics that encourage you to be your best, or do your choices take your mind to places it would be best not to go?

Take a good look at the daily choices you make. What do you allow on your social media pages? Are you selective with your 'friends'? What do you look at on your phone and the internet? How do these choices influence your mind? Take time to think about why you do what you do. I encourage you to not just do what everyone else is doing. Don't be afraid to stand up for what you know is right. You don't have to give an account for others, but God does say that everyone will have to give an account for their own actions.

Do I need to mention the effects of drugs and alcohol? I don't know why our society expects and even encourages young people to drink once they reach the legal age. Think about the long term effects. When you are under the influence, you probably already know that you are much more likely to do things you wouldn't normally do. I would encourage you to stay away from substances that negatively impact your judgment and could lead to harmful consequences. Don't allow friends or someone you are dating influence you to use alcohol or drugs, which can lead to devastating consequences.

I was thinking about a tragic situation which happened in our neighborhood many years ago. Some teenagers got together at a nearby apartment and were drinking. Two of the teenagers got into

a serious argument over a girl. One young man stabbed another young man who died from his wounds. What a terrible waste. If he had lived, I wonder what he would say about his choices that night. His life was cut short because of those choices. The other young man who lived also paid a high price for the choices he made. Both lives were changed in an instant!

The people we choose as our friends can impact our lives in huge ways, either positive or negative. I encourage you to exercise caution when meeting with friends in unfamiliar territory. I would also encourage you to get involved in a church group (or something similar) for young adults, which can provide a safer environment to meet people and make friends. You may want to find a church that challenges you to grow and doesn't simply try to "entertain" you.

I believe the young adult generation has been sold short so many times because we haven't challenged them to do great things. The world has become so obsessed with technology and entertainment that it's easy to lose sight of the needs of others locally and around the world. I think you would love a real challenge if given the opportunity. I believe you are capable of so much more! I encourage you to find ways to go out and make a difference!

"Joy fills hearts that are planning for good!"
Proverbs 12:20

7

Dating

"The Lord grants wisdom! His every work is a treasure of knowledge and understanding. He shows how to distinguish right from wrong, how to find the right decision every time." Proverbs 2:6, 9

"A life of doing right is the wisest life there is. Carry out my instructions; don't forget them, for they will lead you to real living!" Proverbs 4:11, 13

"The man who knows right from wrong and has good judgment and common sense is happier than the man who is immensely rich! Proverbs 3:13

Have you ever found yourself asking "How far is too far?" when it comes to dating and what to allow or not allow? We live in a society that promotes sex as the center of everything. You can hardly look at the television or a billboard and not see that sex is being used to draw your attention to whatever is being sold. I often wonder what advertisers are trying to sell – sex or their products? You are constantly being bombarded with these images if you like it or not.

Because of the influence of the messages we receive from the world, we tend to believe that dating is supposed to be all about sex. A guy takes you out and you're supposed to pay him back by letting him take advantage of you. If you're lucky, he may even convince you that he loves you. But I can almost guarantee that if you give in to him, the relationship will not last very long.

There's a true story in the Bible about a man who was obsessed with his half-sister. He lusted after her until he couldn't take it any longer. He used deceit to lure her to his home where he raped her. She pleaded with him to stop, but he wouldn't. He thought he loved her but once he got what he wanted, his love turned to hatred. He had ruined her reputation in order to satisfy his desires.

I remember one time when I was a teenager and my boyfriend was at my house. My grandma told me he shouldn't come in my bedroom. I thought she was old-fashioned. I wasn't planning to do anything wrong so I didn't see the harm in it. It took me years to see the wisdom in what she said.

Any time you put yourself in a compromising situation or place, you are setting yourself up for trouble. I sometimes think about a family I knew who wouldn't allow their adult children to be in the house alone with someone of the opposite sex. If their parents weren't home, they needed to wait outside or make other plans. That was wisdom.

Group dating is a great idea and provides safety in numbers. Check your goal in dating—is it to get better acquainted with someone or to have sex? A good rule for a man is to think of your date as someone's sister. Think about how you would want a man to treat your sister and then treat your date accordingly. She is also someone's daughter. Some day you may have a daughter. How would you want her to be treated on a date?

I admire a real gentleman. He's the one who opens the door for the lady and walks beside her as her protector (not ahead at a pace she can't keep up with). He treats her with the respect she deserves. He always has her best interests at heart. And he would never think to pressure her to have sex before marriage. Ladies, I know for a fact that there are still some good men out there. You may have to wait awhile, but it will be well worth it when you find the right one!

A while back, I watched a movie titled "One Lucky Lady" with my older grandchildren. It was about a young man who was waiting until marriage for his first kiss. At first, they thought it was pretty

outdated and almost impossible in today's society. But as we watched the movie, they saw wisdom in the idea. This man didn't want to give any part of his heart away before finding the woman he would spend the rest of his life with. He was saving all his affection for that one special lady. I have to ask you ladies - how would you feel if you knew you were the only woman to receive the affections of your husband? Perhaps like one lucky lady?

Are you wondering if this idea is remotely possible today? I know of a young lady who decided to pursue this idea in her life. Growing up she hadn't always made the wisest choices for her life and later realized she didn't like the path she had chosen. So she chose to take a new path. When she found that gentleman I was referring to above, they waited until their wedding day for their first kiss.

Maybe you're saying that it's too late for you. It's never too late to change the course of your life. God is great at giving us second chances (or third, fourth, or whichever one you are on). He is in the business of turning our mistakes into His miracles. I know of another young lady who made an unwise decision and then determined to make wise choices the second time around. She proudly wore white on her wedding day.

Every action leads to a reaction. It starts with holding hands and moves forward from there. If you progress too quickly, all the mystery is gone from the relationship and it probably won't last. Many

men like to date women who don't say "no", but they don't usually choose those same women for marriage partners.

I want to acknowledge the young men who are doing their best to stay pure until marriage. It has always been implied that it's the men who pressure the women to have sex before marriage. I'm not so sure it's that way today. As I see how women present themselves, it's difficult to determine who the purser really is. I encourage you to stay strong – it will be well worth it!

Have you set standards for your dating? Are they specific? If not then you won't know when you've gone too far. I was never told these things when I was growing up. I didn't set up good boundaries and even though I didn't have sex before marriage, I compromised what I believed to be right. It took me many years to forgive myself.

There are some who believe that God made the 10 commandments to keep us from having fun. Actually, the opposite is true. He gave them to protect us from the consequences of our sin. Following His path brings joy, not heartache.

I once saw a very powerful example that I'd like to share with you. You may even want to try it yourself as an experiment. Take two paper hearts and glue them together. Let them dry and then try to take them apart. Just like in real life, you will end up with two torn (broken) hearts.

God didn't design us to give our hearts away on a regular basis. Sex is the 'glue' in a marriage and isn't meant for dating where there is no lifetime commitment. Every time you give away a piece of your heart, you lose another part of yourself. Sex binds you to a person. If you have sex with multiple partners, you can lose the ability to effectively bond with your spouse.

I've never talked to anyone who said they wished they had experienced sex with more partners before marriage, but I have talked to many who wished they had experienced less - especially if they found someone who had kept themselves pure.

Healthy relationships take work—lots of it! You can't always break up and start over. It's best to keep relationships casual until you are ready to think about a serious, lifetime commitment.

There's absolutely nothing wrong with not having a boyfriend or girlfriend. People can put a lot of unnecessary pressure on you by constantly asking who you like or who you're dating. It's okay to just focus on the task ahead of you (like school or a job) without having the pressures of adding another person to your life. There will be plenty of time for that later. Learn to be content with your life whether or not you are in a dating relationship.

The only way to have 'safe sex' is in the confines of marriage. Abstinence works every time! You won't have to worry about getting pregnant before marriage if you aren't having sex. You also don't have to worry about sexually transmitted diseases.

If you have chosen abstinence until marriage, good for you! With so much pressure in today's society, it may seem like you are the only one out there who isn't having sex. It probably hasn't been easy to say no. Others may not realize what a struggle this has been for you, but God sees and He knows. Envision Him smiling down at you, cheering you on!

I would rather be in the minority on the issue of abstinence. You could easily be in the majority if you chose to. But I caution you not to do things you may regret later.

I also want to acknowledge the hurts of those who have been sexually violated in some way. If someone has taken advantage of you or someone you know without consent, my heart breaks for you. I am aware of some pretty painful stories. We live in a very sinful world and because of that, horrible things happen.

But that doesn't mean God isn't concerned or that He doesn't care about you. His heart breaks because of the pain you have experienced. But His choice was to allow us to make our own choices and those choices affect other people. I do know that God can bring restoration in the midst of our deepest hurts.

Don't try to carry that burden alone. Find someone to confide in and ask God to direct you to the help you need. Let Him speak to your heart and remind you how much He loves you. And as you begin to heal, you may be able to help someone

who has gone through a similar situation. I can guarantee there are others who need to hear your story and gain strength from what you learned.

8

For Girls Only

"A beautiful woman lacking discretion and modesty is like a fine gold ring in a pig's snout." Proverbs 11:22

"Charm can be deceptive and beauty doesn't last, but a woman who fears and reverences God shall be greatly praised." Proverbs 31:30

"Don't be concerned about the outward beauty that depends on jewelry, or beautiful clothes, or hair arrangement. Be beautiful inside, in your hearts, with the lasting charm of a gentle and quiet spirit which is so precious to God." 1 Peter 3:3-4

I want to talk to the ladies right now. Have you ever considered how God sees you? He created you to be a unique person with special skills and talents, and He thinks you're beautiful! He created you as one of a kind and He is not only pleased with you, He is very proud of you!

God sees your potential and He delights in you. He wants you to be content with the person He made you to be. He has a plan for your life which may include a man who loves you (I say 'may' because marriage isn't in everyone's future). I encourage you to value yourself and not settle for anything less.

We've all seen countless magazines and women in movies who, because of air-brushing, look flawless. They appear to be the perfect size and shape. There's no way anyone could ever measure up to that. We forget that the model's outer beauty may not reflect what is in her heart. Outer beauty fades over time.

What do people see when they look at you? What kind of words come out when you speak? I have seen women who are extremely beautiful by worldly standards, but when they open their mouth, the words that come out make their beauty quickly fade.

I have also seen women who would not be called "beautiful" according to the world's standards, but their words and actions shine so brightly that they appear beautiful to everyone they meet. Think about the kind of woman you want to be. Our countenance and our words reflect what is in our heart. What do your countenance and your words reveal about the condition of your heart?

I'd like to address fashions in this chapter. Is your clothing sexy and revealing, or modest yet stylish? Take an honest look in the mirror. The way we dress expresses how we want others to see us.

I feel embarrassed for women when I see them wearing clothing that is too revealing. My first thought is to find something to cover them up. Maintaining a sense of modesty and mystery is more flattering than exposing to others what is under your clothing. Too many of today's clothing manufacturers have turned women's fashions into a public display. It seems as though Victoria forgot how to keep a secret. If you dress in this manner, you may be tempted to compromise on your boundaries.

What would you rather have a man attracted to - what he is envisioning under your clothes, or the beauty inside your heart? I'm not saying that we don't need to take care of ourselves and of our appearance. But I think it's always good to remember that what's on the outside will fade over time. If you cultivate inner beauty in your heart, those qualities will never fade. They actually grow more beautiful over time.

I heard once about a youth group that had a discussion about the manner in which the girls dressed. Some of the young men wrote letters which were read to the girls explaining how their suggestive clothing made it difficult for them to stay pure in their thoughts and actions.

I think it would be helpful for girls to hear that. If you want to marry a good man, you need to do your part. That includes dressing in a way that will help him keep his thoughts pure and respectful towards you. It's possible to dress modestly and still be stylish. I'd love to see it more often. Choose to make a fashion statement to other women by dressing in less revealing ways. You might even start a new trend!

Okay guys, I know you are reading this chapter too. Do you agree with me?

For Guys Only

"Follow the steps of the godly, and stay on the right path, for only good men enjoy life to the full." Proverbs 2:20-21

"Be with wise men and become wise. Be with evil men and become evil." Proverbs 13:20

"Before every man there lies a wide and pleasant road that seems right but ends in death." Proverbs 14:12

"Kindness makes a man attractive." Proverbs 19:22

I'd like you to consider your appearance and the message you are sending to the ladies. Do your clothes (especially your pants) fit or are they falling off of you? It's not very appealing to the rest of us to have to look at your boxers.

I admire the many men who dress appropriately. Dressing nicely doesn't have to cost a lot of money. We notice when you take the time to look presentable and we appreciate your efforts!

I have seen young men's vehicles that have bumper stickers or other things attached which have made it very clear what their intentions were. I would be cautious (maybe even fearful) to even get in that vehicle with the man behind the wheel. Have you seen any of the vehicles I'm talking about? Is it possible that you own one of them? I do have to admit, I'd rather have you advertise your intentions than to not know and regret my decision to go out with you.

Make wise choices. How are you presenting yourself to the world? What word would best describe you? Are you respectful of women or do you use them for your own pleasure? Are you abusive or kind? What kind of words come out of your mouth?

What comes to your mind when you think of women? Where do your thoughts go and what is your goal for a date? You may have been given the impression that sex is the reason for dating. I'd like to encourage you to change your end goal.

God obviously created women differently from men. He did that for a reason. Women were created

to be man's helper and companion. God has great plans for you regarding sex, but He has reserved it for marriage only.

By now, you already know how babies are conceived. It's not my intention to address that with you. Probably the biggest question is, are you ready for the responsibility of a child at this point in your life? There are too many children in the world who don't know their fathers. You may even be one of them. Some men may not care that they created a baby who now needs a mom and a dad (and someone to support them).

Our society is struggling today because too many men aren't taking responsibility for their choices. They seem to be more concerned with their own pleasure. Children are God's most amazing gift and they were meant to be enjoyed by two parents who love each other. That's why God says that marriage is the only safe place for sex to happen.

A woman's desire is to be loved and treated with respect by a man. She wants you to be her knight in shining armor. I don't believe women are looking for someone to use them to fulfill their desires. They may give in to you, hoping to find love. But I ask you not to lead them down that path. Step up and be a man of integrity who makes wise choices. We need more of you out there.

What do you think ladies? I know you read this one too. Keep those men accountable. They will love you for it!

10

College and Career

"I will instruct you (says the Lord) and guide you along the best pathway for your life; I will advise you and watch your progress." Psalms 32:8

"In everything you do, put God first, and He will direct you and crown your efforts with success." Proverbs 3:6

Many of you have gone or will be going to college one day. Do you know that God wants to have a say in what school you choose and what career you pursue? Have you thought to ask Him

what the best choice is for you? He knows the talents and the desires in your heart because He put them there. Because of that, He wants you to do all you can to grow in those areas and be all that He created you to be.

College is a time of newfound freedom, especially if you move away from home and are making your own decisions and setting your own boundaries. Just because you're on your own, it would be best not to throw all the rules you have learned out the window. If you do, I believe you will regret it.

You will most likely be faced with many new pressures like drinking, partying and of course, having sex. Many of you may have already experimented with those things. Though they may seem fun for a while, remember that the choices you make now will affect the rest of your life. Are you willing to trade momentary pleasures for a lifetime of consequences?

If you haven't built a good foundation in your life prior to being on your own, there is a very good chance that you will be easily swayed by the masses. That's why it's so important to choose your friends wisely! It's best to find friends who will help you stay strong when temptations come against you.

Know what you believe and take a stand for it. That way you won't come out weaker on the other side. You will grow stronger. Choose carefully what you put in your mind and in your heart. Be the friend who helps others make good choices too.

If you are in a career, do you encourage and lift up your fellow employees or do you consider your job more of a competition? God will make sure you get the promotions you deserve if you keep your focus on helping others succeed at their work. It's best to keep the focus off yourself and watch what God does!

⟨11⟩

Cohabitation?

"Above all else, guard your affections. For they influence everything else in your life." Proverbs 4:23

You may be thinking "What's the matter with living together? We love each other and plan to get married—someday. Besides, we need to try this out and make sure we are compatible."

We used to have a saying, "Who wants to buy a pair of shoes without trying them on?" My response would be, "Who wants to buy a used pair of shoes?"

If we check the statistics, couples who start out by living together before marriage greatly reduce their chances of being happily married and staying together. The problem is that living in the same

house is still much like dating. You are still putting your best foot forward.

Marriage does something inside of you. You finally let down and become the person you really are. For many people, living together before marriage has become the normal progression in relationships today, but I'm holding firm in my conviction that cohabitation is not God's best for you.

I'm sure you could tell me about some instances where couples who lived together prior to marriage have stayed together for a long time. I would guess that in most of these cases, God has become part of the relationship at some point along the way. Honestly, I don't know how marriages survive the things that come against them without God at the center of their relationship.

Let's take a good, hard look at the facts. If you truly desire a lifelong relationship, is there any reason why you wouldn't want to start out right—with the wedding ring first? Is there something keeping you from a marriage commitment? If one of you is resisting making this commitment, is it possible you are only looking for a roommate with benefits instead of a forever partner?

I have one final thought on this subject. When you get married, do you want to go on a honeymoon or just a vacation? A honeymoon is the proper time to explore the gift of sex with your forever partner, not just take a trip with someone you have already given yourself to. What if the person you choose has saved himself or herself just for you? Would you want to give that same gift back to them if possible?

⟨12⟩

Marriage

"Don't be teamed with those who do not love the Lord, for what do the people of God have in common with the people of sin? How can light live with darkness? How can a Christian be a partner with one who doesn't believe?" 1 Corinthians 6:14-15

I'm pretty sure I would be correct to assume that most of you plan to get married someday. Have you ever stopped to think about the qualities you would look for in a mate?

I used to get together with a group of girls and we spent some time discussing this topic. I asked them to write out the things they would look for in a

marriage partner. You may want to do this yourself as a starting place.

Here some things I would suggest looking for:

How does the person you are interested in get along with their family members (and with yours)? Girls, how does he treat his mother and sisters? Guys, what does she think of her father and brothers? How do they treat her? How do they view and talk about the opposite sex?

How do they drive in traffic? Do the words "road rage" come to mind? This may give you some good insight into behaviors that could emerge later.

Do they hold grudges and talk mostly about the faults they see in others, or are they quick to forgive and always looking for the best in people?

Do you seem to get along well or do you have frequent fights? If the fighting is typical, that will magnify in a marriage. Many times marriage can reveal the worst in us.

How do they treat people such as waiters or store clerks? Are they content to wait their turn or are they impatient, demanding that their needs be put above others who are also waiting?

When a stressful situation arises, do they take it in stride (and maybe even laugh about it), or is their first reaction anger or retaliation?

Is this person overly protective, or not wanting you to spend time with your family or friends? This is not a good sign. Proceed with caution. Or better yet, proceed right out the door while you still can.

What do your family members and friends think of the person you have chosen? If they are concerned, listen to what they have to say. They may be seeing things that you haven't even noticed. Keep an open mind.

Does the person respect you? Have they been faithful to you in the dating relationship or do their eyes seem to stray?

Try to date the person for a full year, through all the seasons. You can only pretend to be someone you're not for so long. Behaviors will eventually come out into the light.

Take your faith into consideration. If you are a follower of Jesus Christ, it isn't wise to marry someone who doesn't share your beliefs. You could have a hard road ahead of you. It's very difficult to build an intimate relationship with someone who doesn't share the choices and desires of your heart.

I saved the most important consideration for last. Ask God to show you the person who is His very best pick for you. He would love to guide you in this decision. This is one big area where He really wants to have the final say. And you'll be so glad you asked!

Since dating leads to marriage, these questions are also good to ask yourself about the people you choose to date. Every date has the potential of becoming a marriage partner so you should choose carefully who you go out with. It would be best to consider these qualities from a distance whenever

possible, before the emotions become strong and it's harder to be impartial to the facts.

This list is not exhaustive and I realize that no one is perfect. But if you sense too many of these 'red flags', take a step back and ask someone you trust to help you evaluate your relationship. Don't move forward without giving much thought to your concerns. Even if you are already engaged and the marriage is planned (for tomorrow!), it's not too late to change your mind. It would be better to be a little embarrassed by calling off a marriage than to make such a huge commitment. I guarantee that the guests will understand (and maybe even admire you for having the courage to do so). I'm not talking about the 'butterflies' you may experience before marriage. I think you understand the difference of what I'm talking about.

You shouldn't go into marriage thinking you can change the other person. The only one you can change is YOU. If you don't like who they are now, before marriage, it's better to move on before you make a lifetime commitment. Even though people can change, it's much more realistic to begin a marriage content with who this person is right now, not who you hope they will become.

I think I also need to say that once you are married, you need to stop looking at the above list and the faults in your spouse that you may have missed. Once you have made your commitment, stay focused on the good things you find in your

partner, not the things that they do wrong (or differently from you).

Some young adults may be so anxious to marry that they possibly don't stop to consider what they are committing to—a lifetime of together. That can be many, many (many!) years! Make sure you enjoy being around the person A LOT before you commit to marriage.

I question how many couples take time to consider just what they are saying when they speak their marriage vows. I have lived through 'for better or for worse, for richer or for poorer, in sickness and in health' for quite a few years now. Marriage can be one of the most challenging, yet most rewarding, relationships you will be in. It takes work—lots of it. I think God made it that way so we wouldn't take each other for granted.

I'm not trying to discourage you from getting married. I just want you to see past the fairytale, "happily ever after" ending. We have all seen enough marriages in our lifetimes that haven't ended well. I'm pretty sure you don't want to be another statistic. Instead, strive to be an example of what a really good marriage can look like. Determine ahead of time to stay together no matter what. I'm not talking about abusive relationships. Those need to be dealt with swiftly.

I want to encourage you that if you follow the right guidelines and find someone who truly loves you, you can have a fulfilling marriage that lasts through the ups and downs of life.

Love isn't a feeling that comes and goes. We hear of so many marriages that have ended because one spouse "fell out of love" with the other. But in reality, love is a choice. We can choose to stay when the feelings aren't as strong. If we do stay and determine to focus on whatever is positive (even if it's just the smallest thing), our feelings will change.

If you run every time your feelings shift, you will undoubtedly experience a lifetime of disappointments. I encourage you to choose to love, regardless of what message your feelings are sending you.

No one can fulfill all of your needs. You have to be secure in who you are and not expect another person to be all that you need. Only God can do that. Know who you are before you bring another person into the picture.

Marriage is one of God's gifts to us. When we follow His blueprints, our lives and our relationships can be life-giving instead of life-taking. Instead of draining all of our energy, marriage can give us strength because we have someone to stand with us. But we have to be willing to follow His plans and not our own. God makes all the difference! A cord of three strands is not easily broken.

Forgiveness

"Your heavenly Father will forgive you if you forgive those who sin against you; but if you refuse to forgive them, He will not forgive you." Matthew 6:14-15

"Do for others what you want them to do for you." Matthew 7:12

I would be doing you an injustice to leave out this chapter. This is another huge foundation stone and the key to so many other issues in life. At first glance the above verse may seem pretty harsh, so let me try to explain. If you make the choice to withhold forgiveness from others, God won't forgive you. That's pretty straightforward. One of the reasons is because unforgiveness will bring about many heartaches in your own life.

Jesus freely gave His life so your sins could be forgiven—completely, in full - with nothing left that would separate you from Him. But we block that forgiveness if we refuse to forgive others when they do wrong against us. If we took a good, hard look at our own lives, we would probably have to admit that we don't deserve the kind of total, complete forgiveness that Jesus offers. But He offers it anyway because He loves us. His expectation is that we freely forgive others out of gratitude for all the ways we have been forgiven.

We can't expect mercy and forgiveness from God and then demand justice from others for their wrongdoing. That's not how it works. If we demand justice then God will also demand it of us. We are given the choice of justice or mercy, and whichever one we choose will come back upon us.

Forgiveness doesn't mean letting the other person off the hook for what they did or didn't do. It means that you turn them over to God, allowing Him to do any correcting that needs to be done and trusting that His ways are always best.

If we refuse to forgive, it's like drinking poison and hoping the other person dies. It does much more damage to you than it does to the other person. If you choose the road of unforgiveness, it can literally destroy your life. The best choice is to live free, allowing God to fight your battles for you.

What If?

What if everything I told you is true? And what if everything God says in the Bible is also true? How would that change your life if you let it?

What if you chose to believe with childlike faith and follow God with all your heart, soul and mind? What would that look like? What kind of an impact could that have on every relationship you are in? What about in the world?

What if you believed that God has a specific plan for your life that only you can fulfill? What if you asked Him to show you that plan and then ran after it for all you're worth? What if you accomplished His

purposes for you? What and who would be eternally changed because of it? And how would it change you?

What if Jesus is really coming back to earth (which He is!) to gather up all those who not only believe in Him, but know Him personally? And what if He is coming soon (in your lifetime)? What if He takes you home with Him? What if He doesn't?

What if you lived your life to the fullest extent? What if you practiced kindness every day of your life? What if you chose to be a leader and not a follower? What if you stood up for what is right and stopped following the crowd? What if you influenced others to be the best they could be?

What if you really believed you could choose your final destiny? Would you choose heaven and do all God calls you to do and be, or would you easily go to hell by default (Sometimes by not choosing, the choice is made for us.)?

What if you found a church that teaches the radical truths of Jesus and joined forces with other believers? What if together you could make a big difference by standing against the evil all around you?

What if heaven is your final home and you can take people there with you (as many as you want!)? What if the eternal rewards are totally worth pursuing, but we only have this life to accumulate them?

What if you got serious about God? With all my heart, I pray that you will.

Conclusion

"Therefore, if any man is in Christ, he is a new creature; the old things passed away; behold, new things have come." 2 Corinthians 5:17

"A man who refuses to admit his mistakes can never be successful. But if he confesses and forsakes them, he gets another chance." Proverbs 28:13

"I call heaven and earth to witness against you today, that I have set before you life and death, the blessing and the curse. So choose life in order that you may live, you and your descendants, by loving

the Lord your God, by obeying His voice, and by holding fast to Him." Deuteronomy 30:19-20

"What happiness for those whose guilt has been forgiven! What joy when sins are covered over! What relief for those who have confessed their sins and God has cleared their record." Psalms 32:1-2

It doesn't matter where you find yourself in life at this moment because it's never too late for a new beginning. It's a new day and you can choose to begin again. So many times I feel like I need a fresh start—again! God is the God of second chances! You are never beyond hope in His eyes!

I have talked a lot about choices. Every choice you make matters for eternity. We don't just live this life and then we die. We can actually do things in this life which God will reward us for in heaven. These rewards don't rust and fade like the ones we receive down here on earth. These rewards last for eternity.

I have touched on choices in many areas. If you want to begin or continue to make good choices, you will need help from God who has all the right answers and is more than willing to share these answers with you.

In this life we all have many questions. Jesus is the only One who can help you discover all the right answers. Jesus is the only One who can help you

live those answers once you find them. And Jesus is the only One who will stay by your side through all the choices of your life.

Who do you say that Jesus is? This is the most important question you will ever have to answer. Some day we will each have to answer that question for ourselves. He desires to be so much more than someone you know casually. He wants you to know Him intimately, like He knows you. Take a moment to consider that the God who created the whole universe wants to be your friend! What could ever compare to that?

The answer to this question (and so many more) can be found in the Bible. I encourage you to open the Book and find the answers for yourself. God's tests are always "open book" because He doesn't want you to fail!

God is the source of all wisdom. I can't say enough that HE LOVES YOU, more than you could ever imagine!! He wants you to succeed in this life. He isn't looking to punish you when you do wrong. He's there to lift you up and put you back on your feet when you fail and need a new beginning. And He never gets tired of picking you up! He believes in you! Sometimes we may feel like giving up on ourselves but God never gives up on us. He continually pursues us with His love.

God will never force Himself on anyone. We have to personally make the decision to trust Him with our lives and believe He will do all that He

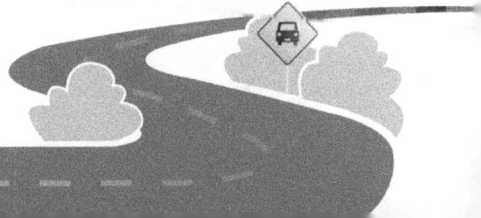

promises. The other choice is to continue to live life separated from God. Your choice can be the starting point on a road to freedom by deciding to follow God's way or choosing a life of bondage by insisting on your own choices.

God loved you enough to send His only Son to die in your place, so why would He withhold any good thing from you? God loves you and He is for you!! His desire is to pick you up, dust you off, and set your feet on a firm foundation. He wants to be your best friend! His friendship is nothing like what the world offers you. He would never hurt you.

Many times we get discouraged when God doesn't answer our prayers in the way we would like Him to. God is a really good parent. I'm guessing that your parents don't always give you everything you want - especially if they really love you. Although we don't always know what is best for us, God knows and He won't give you anything that isn't the very best. That's another good reason to thank Him when life doesn't go as you had planned.

God loves it when we talk to Him all throughout the day. We call it prayer, but it's as simple as having a conversation with Him like you would with your best friend. You can be completely honest with God because He already knows all about you.

Don't let the idea of praying to God intimidate you. Many people have turned prayer into a list of rules that need to be followed in order to get the desired results. We can be so afraid of not expressing

ourselves correctly that we don't even make the attempt. God is delighted when we take the time to talk to Him. God loves **your** prayers! And the best part is, if you take time to listen instead of doing all the talking, He will speak to you as well.

I'm still amazed every time He answers me! I don't know why I should be surprised but I am. Maybe' awed' would be a better word. It seems pretty amazing that the God who created the whole universe take time to talk to you and me!

Many times new believers in Christ seem to receive answers more quickly. I think God does that to encourage them in their newfound faith. As you grow in your faith, you may find that you need to listen more closely. If we get too busy with life and the many distractions that come our way, we may not stop long enough to listen for God's still, small voice.

When I was considering whether I should write this book, I asked God whether or not He wanted me to proceed. His answer was immediate. I opened a devotional of mine and read "Don't you think it's time for you to tell those people the Good News about Jesus Christ? Aren't you glad someone told you? They may not act thrilled when you first approach them, but after a while the message will begin to sink in, and they'll be so thankful you told them the Good News!" I took that as a 'YES'. I love it when God makes Himself so clear!

At some point in each day you may want to turn off your cell phone (yes, even the cell phone),

your computer, the music and anything else that is calling for your attention. The world can wait. Would you be surprised if I told you that we didn't even have cell phones when I was your age and we managed to live through it? And I remember that life wasn't so hectic then.

The Bible is another really good place to hear God speaking to you. Everything we own has instructions included. Think of the Bible as God's instruction manual for your life. It contains the most important instructions you will ever follow.

When you begin to read the Bible, you may not want to start reading at the beginning or you may quickly get discouraged. But as you grow in your faith, I encourage you not to leave out the Old Testament. It's full of people the world considered failures and many of them did some pretty horrific things, but God used them greatly because they believed in the second chance.

I would suggest that you start in the New Testament with the Gospels (Matthew, Mark, Luke and John). You may also want to add the Psalms (David was very honest with his feelings in the Psalms) and Proverbs (they are full of wisdom that will guide you). You will also want to get a translation that you are comfortable with and can understand. You may need to ask someone to help direct you.

The Bible is God's love letter to you. We all like to receive love letters (at least I know I do). God inspired the writers of His Book (the Bible) so we

would be encouraged in our journey of life. The stories are true and the parables are to teach us more truths. If you read with your mind open to all that is written there, it will change your life if you choose to let it!

I have included many references from the Bible in this book to give you a glimpse of what is there and to hopefully draw you in further. I could have listed hundreds more but I'd rather have you search for them yourself. They are so exciting and encouraging that it was hard for me to know when to stop!

We don't get to pick and choose what we want to believe from the Bible and what we want to throw out. It's all or nothing.

God is still writing things down in His Book. He is keeping a record of all that we say and do. He can give the worst story the most beautiful ending ever! You are in that Book. Your daily choices will determine how your ending will read.

"Oh, put God to the test and see how kind He is! See for yourself the way His mercies shower down on all who trust in Him." Psalms 34:8

"For all God's words are right, and everything He does is worthy of our trust." Psalm 33:4

Heaven is a very real place. So is hell. And guess what? You get to choose which one will be your eternal home. No one else can make that choice for you. And since eternity is a very long time, it would be good to take time to get all the facts so you can make your decision wisely!

You may have been told that you need to be a good person and do certain things to get into Heaven (like go to church, keep the commandments, be nice to people, etc). The problem is that you can't be good enough or do enough good things to get to heaven on your own. Hell is easy to enter, but not so with Heaven.

"Heaven can be entered only through the narrow gate! The highway to hell is broad, and its gate is wide enough for all the multitudes who choose its easy way. But the Gateway to Life is small, and the road is narrow, and only a few ever find it." Matthew 7:13-14

In other words, choosing hell is easy. If you choose hell, you will have eternity to think about the choices you made that got you there. And there's no way out.

Heaven is the other choice. Again, Jesus knew you couldn't get there on your own merit because you are a sinner. That's why He came to die for you. He lived the sinless life that you couldn't so you

could put on His righteousness and enter Heaven. When God, the Father, looks at you, He sees what His Son, Jesus, did. And He is pleased. All of your sins and failures are blotted out forever!

I was thinking about God's refining process in us and how He "chips away" the parts that may hurt us (if we let Him). Every time He removes something, I think it leaves a 'hole' in us. The more chipping away He does, the more "holes" He leaves. Then I realized that when we have "holes", He has a chance to shine through because parts of us have been removed. Maybe that's a glimpse of what it means to be "holy".

I can't wrap this up without telling you how you can receive the hope that I have. I am a precious princess! I am a child of God (it says so in God's love letter to me—the Bible)! I have the assurance that when I die, I will spend eternity in heaven.

These same things can be true of you, but you have to choose them. You do this by asking God to be your Father. His desire is to make you His son or daughter. He is beyond any father that you have known in your life. He will make you His child and clothe you with His righteousness. He will clean you up and make you "holy" as you pursue Him. Remember that you can never be good enough on your own, but with Christ living in you, you can look just like Him. That's pretty amazing!!

It all starts with a simple prayer. You can use mine as a guide. God loves your heartfelt prayers!

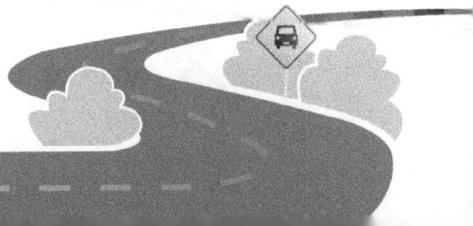

Dear God,

I have made a mess of my life and I need Your help. I ask You to forgive me for all the ways I have disobeyed Your perfect plans for me. I thank You for bringing me to this point and for everything and everyone who has had a part in leading me here. I know I can't do life your way without Your help, so I ask you to come and live inside me. Remove the things that hurt Your heart so You can shine through me. Help me to change any wrong ways of thinking and learn to respond as You would in every situation I am confronted with in my life. Make me 'holy' and wholly Yours. I love you, Jesus. Thank you for taking the punishment for my sin so I can live with You forever. Amen

If you sincerely prayed this prayer (or your own), God accepts you as His child, and He will bring you safely through this life to the next one. And now you can move forward and live the life He planned for you.

I would love to see more who would encourage you to stand firm in your conviction to do the right thing. I believe you are worth it. I believe you are capable of living with high standards that will not only protect your body but your heart also.

I want you to know that God believes in you. I am praying for you and cheering you on, even if I don't know you personally. You are a very special generation and my heart yearns for you to know the truths that will set you free.

"What pity Jesus felt for the crowds that came, because their problems were so great and they didn't know what to do or where to go for help." Matthew 9:36

God cares about your life and your situation, whatever it is. I care about you and I know there are many others who feel the same way. Ask God to lead you to the people who are eagerly waiting to help you.

You only live twice – the life you are living right now and the one you will live forever. I plead with you to consider God and His ways. Make wise choices. And I pray that I will meet you in heaven one day. Until then, may God bless and keep you in His care.

More books by YOLT Publishing

The Power of a Dream—*This story is about how God brought two totally different people together to change a little piece of the world.*

YOLT: You Only Live Twice—*Have you ever considered that everything you do in this first life has an eternal impact on the second life? You only live twice so it's wise to think about what you are living for. There's too much at stake to live life without purpose.*

YOLT Junior: You Only Live Twice—*Don't be afraid to dream big. With God's help you can accomplish great things. Your life matters regardless of your age.*

www.YOLTPublishing.com

www.ingramcontent.com/pod-product-compliance
Lightning Source LLC
Chambersburg PA
CBHW071929020426
42331CB00010B/2783